Your Inner Six-Year-Old

S0-BRA-199

Your Inner Six-Year-Old

Change Your Life Forever

REM JACKSON

Illustrations by
ANNIE JACKSON

Stonebrook Publishing
Saint Louis, Missouri

STONEBROOK
PUBLISHING

A STONEBROOK PUBLISHING BOOK
©2020 Rem Jackson and Annie Jackson

All rights reserved. Published in the United States by Stonebrook Publishing,
a division of Stonebrook Enterprises, LLC, Saint Louis, Missouri.
No part of this book may be reproduced, scanned, or distributed in any
printed or electronic form without written permission from the author.

Please do not participate in or encourage piracy
of copyrighted materials in violation of the author's rights.

ISBN: 978-1-7347340-5-8

Dedicated to
the precious inner six-year-old in us all.

Life can be complex, frustrating, and difficult. Or simple and blessed.
Sometimes it seems like they are both at the same time.
So much depends on your inner life and mindset.

There is no point in rehashing the past because it no longer exists, and there is no point in worrying about the future because it never comes. You can only live in the present moment, and when you do, you have a decent chance for a life filled with grace, peace, and happiness.

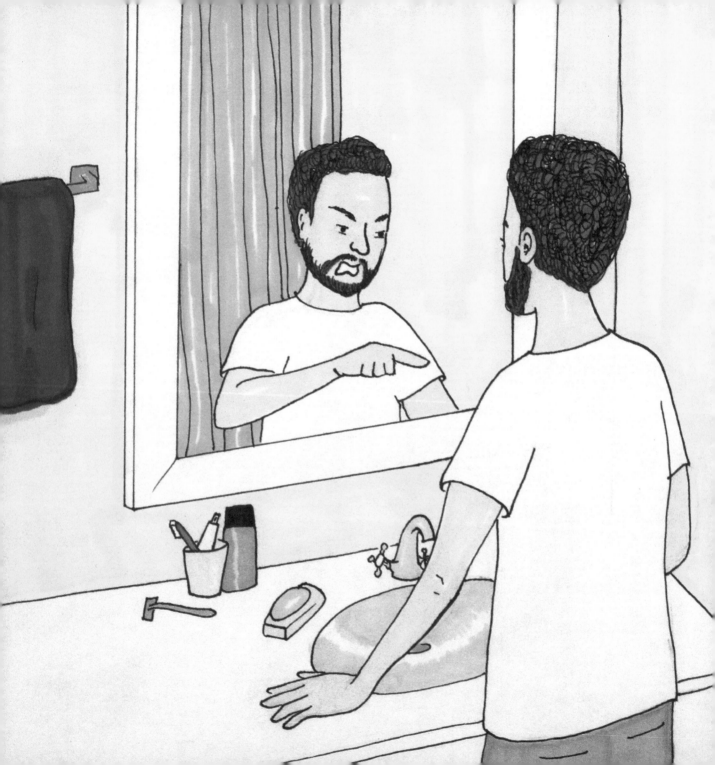

Who talks trash to you? The really nasty stuff—the words that pack a psychological blow to the gut? Most likely it is not the people you work with. They are far too skilled to openly beat you up. Not your family (hopefully), at least not directly. Those messages, if they do come, can produce guilt, but they are not the really horrible stuff.

Nope. You are the only one who can take yourself out to the woodshed for a real beating. No one can grind your soul into dust like you can do to yourself.

We are all guilty of this, and some of us are fantastically gifted in this category.

Ask yourself why. Why do you do that to yourself? What did you do that was so bad that you deserve to be psychologically beaten? And make no mistake, that's what this is, a steady drumbeat of abuse from the one person you can't get away from no matter how hard you try: YOU.

This weekend, wouldn't it be fun if you could spend the day with yourself as a six-year-old? You could drive up to your old house and there you would be on the porch, ready for you to pull up in the car.

You would run up and jump into the car, buckle your seatbelt, and with great anticipation, look over at the grown-up ready to hang out with you. Your adult self would look into the eyes of this precious child and ask, "Well, Remy, what would you like to do today?" Of course, you would already know the secrets of this little child's heart, and when your six-year-old-self answered, you would reply, "I thought you might say that. Let's go!"

As you spent the day with this lovely child, how would you talk to him? You might try to teach him all about investments and suggest some great stock tips; you might even try to teach him how to access the funds to accomplish the trades. But this six-year-old would be lost, so you would soon abandon that plan. You might tell him not to go out with a specific girl on a certain night, so he could avoid two years of heartache in the future, but this plan would most likely fail as well.

What you would not do is berate and belittle this child. You would not hit this little boy on the forehead and call him stupid. You would not tell him that he "always does this!" You would not wake this precious little child up in the middle of the night and pound him with blow after blow of a parade of his mistakes. You would not repeat the litany of things you were told were wrong with you throughout your life by your family and friends. You would not look at him in disgust for being too short, tall, fat, skinny, average, and more. You would not attack him incessantly with a well-rehearsed list of his shortcomings.

Instead, you would nurture and cherish this little soul. You would tell him how great he is. How much you love him. You would tell him about some of the wonderful blessings that will come his way. If you could, you would tell him about his own children and how wonderful they will be, how he will flourish in his career and how proud he'll be of that achievement. If you could, you would tell this little child about the blessings that will rain down upon him.

You would tell him that you love him and that he will make mistakes in his life—many—but that he should not be hard on himself when it happens. You would tell him that every time he made a mistake, he meant to do the right thing. He tried to be the best person he could. And you would tell him that he's a wonderful person worthy of love and respect.

And you would say that **you will always be with him—every minute of every day—and you will help and guide him. You will always be there for him and you will never let him down.** And you would tell him that you love him. Many times.

This little six-year-old would look deep in your eyes and believe every word you say. Just like the adult you are today believes every word you say.

So, the next time you take yourself out to the woodshed, stop. Remember to speak to yourself as though you are that six-year-old. Resolve to never again inflict pain and suffering on yourself. Shrink yourself down to a little six-year-old and look into those eyes before you speak to yourself. You will find yourself saying, "It's OK. You weren't trying to mess that up. Let's fix it. It's not that bad. You are a wonderful person, worthy of love and respect."

Keep your promise to that little six-year-old you. Be your own best friend each and every day. Nurture your own spirit and mind and body. Turn to yourself as your number one source of support.

Celebrate the blessings you have. They are great and many. Stop and smell the roses every time you walk past them.

If you nurture your own spirit, you'll have an almost limitless capacity to help and love others.

Nurture your inner six-year-old, and you can change your life forever.

REM JACKSON is the father of three daughters and has been married to his beloved Diane for thirty years. He has been caring for his inner six-year-old every day for over ten years. In his spare time, he is the CEO of Top Practices, the author of *Podiatry Prosperity: Market, Manage, and Love your Practice*, and the host of the podcast "Prosperity and Something Greater."

ANNIE JACKSON, one of Rem's three daughters, is an artist and entrepreneur. She is the creator of This is Brennan, an eco-friendly company that produces unique naturally-dyed pieces in which the colors come from plant materials like onion skins, avocado pits, and more. When she is not dyeing, illustrating, or building a business, she is often traveling the world with her husband.

For more information about this book,
including how to buy multiple copies in bulk, go to
www.YourInnerSixYearOld.com

CPSIA information can be obtained
at www.ICGtesting.com
Printed in the USA
LVHW050746170920
666168LV00004B/14